MIKWITE'LMANEJ MIKMAQI'K

LET US REMEMBER THE OLD MI'KMAQ

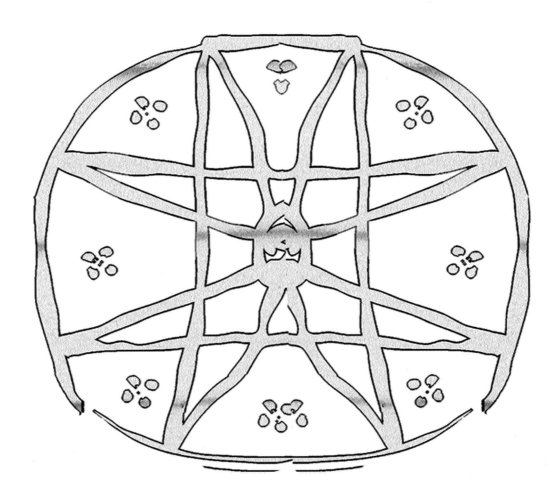

Based on an exhibition of the same name produced by
The Confederacy of Mainland Mi'kmaq, Truro, Nova Scotia, and the
Robert S. Peabody Museum of Archaeology, Phillips Academy, Andover, Massachusetts

Nimbus Publishing Limited
PO Box 9166, Halifax, NS   B3K 5M8
(902) 455-4286

Printed and bound in Canada

Canadian Cataloguing in Publication Data

The Robert S. Peabody Museum of Archaeology, Andover
        Mikwite'lmanej Mikmaqi'k=Let us remember the old Mi'kmaq

Exhibition of photographs curated by The Confederacy of Mainland Mi'kmaq, Truro (Nova Scotia) and the Robert S. Peabody Museum of Archaeology, Phillips Academy, Andover (Massachusetts)

Text in English, with t.p. and preface in English and Mi'kmaq.
        ISBN 1-55109-350-2

1. Micmac Indians—History—20th century—Pictorial works. 2. Micmac Indians—Exhibitions. 3. Robert S. Peabody Museum of Archaeology—Exhibitions. I. Johnson, Frederick, 1904-1994 II. Rosenmeier, Leah III. Bernard, Tim IV. Martin, Catherine V. Confederacy of Mainland Mi'kmaq (Micmacs). VI. Title. VII. Title: Let us remember the old Mi'kmaq.

TR647.J63 2001   971.5'004973   C00-901708-9
Hardcover edition: ISBN 1-55109-390-1

 Canadian   Patrimoine
Heritage   canadien

Funded by Museums Assistance Programme, Department of Canadian Heritage
Financement: Programme d'aide aux musées, ministere du Patrimoine canadien

Nimbus acknowledges the financial support of the Government of Canada through the Book Publishing Industry Development Program (BPIDP) and the Canada Council for our publishing activities.

A Note on Transliteration

During the course of this project, the Mi'kmaw translation of *Let Us Remember the Old Mi'kmaq* changed from *Mikwitemanej Mikmanaqi'k* to *Miwite'lmanej Mikmaqi'k*. Because only a small number of speakers write Mi'kmaq, transliteration continues to be a dynamic process. The changes in the title reflect ongoing conversations among those speakers who wish to capture the spoken word on paper. A number of Mi'kmaw speakers and advisors, Patsy Paul Martin and Murdena Marshall primarily, summarized the English text in Mi'kmaq. Murdena and Patsy worked also with Helen Sylliboy and Dianna Denny in arriving at the translations. Thank you to Katherine Sorbey for her assistance with the title of this book. Sustaining and increasing the use of Mi'kmaq continues to be a priority for Mi'kmaw people.

Welcome

Wela'liek

To the Elders whose voices made this book and the exhibition on
which it is based possible, we are grateful for your stories and wisdom.

Alma Benoit

Aloysius Benoit

Leonard Bernard

Mary E. Brooks

Raymond Cope

Saqamaw Albert Denny

Frank Denny Sr.

Martha Denny

Mary Ellen Denny

Raymond Francis

Sarah Francis

Dennis Gloade Sr. (1926-1999)

Annie Claire Googoo

Caroline Gould

Marjorie Gould

Mary Rose Gould

Roddie J. Gould

John Nick Jeddore

Saqamaw Mi'sel Joe

Madeline John

Alexander Julien

Don Julien

Frank Julien (1927-2000)

Albert Marshall

Annie Tena Marshall

Caroline Marshall

Lillian B. Marshall

Murdena Marshall

Bennett Martin

Jean Martin

Ken Martin

Madeline Martin

Molly McDonald

Nancy S. Morris

John M. Prosper (1922-2000)

Wilfred Prosper

Doris Sapier

Fred Sapier

Levi Stride

Catherine Thomas

Wela'liek

Along with the Elders who shared their stories, The Confederacy of Mainland Mi'kmaq and the Robert S. Peabody Museum wish to express their gratitude to the following people and organizations who have contributed to the production of this book:

Firstly, to our Ancestors–the many Mi'kmaw Chiefs and Elders–who have gone before us. It is with their wisdom, love and foresight that we as the Mi'kmaq are able to share these lovely images with you;

to Mr. Frederick Johnson (1904-1994) for capturing this piece of history to share forever;

to Cyndi Martin and Albert Marshall who helped lead these photos to us;

to the project team, especially Murdena Marshall and Don Julien, who provided continuous guidance;

to Saqamaw Mi'sel Joe who worked with us on Miawpukek history and genealogy;

to Patsy Paul-Martin for her Mi'kmaw translation;

to Sara Germain for her editorial expertise and enthusiasm;

to the Museum Assistance Program of the Department of Canadian Heritage for its generous funding of this book. The Massachusetts Foundation for the Humanities, the Maine Humanities Council, the Nova Scotia Arts Council, and Sable Offshore Energy Inc., provided critical support of the exhibition *Mikwite'lmanej Mikmaqi'k: Let Us Remember the Old Mi'kmaq,* upon which this book is based;

to the staff of Eastern Woodland Publishing for their cooperation, patience, and design expertise;

to James W. Bradley and the staff of the Robert S. Peabody Museum for their support;

to Cathy Martin for sharing the many gifted skills with which she is blessed;

to Tim Bernard, the propelling force behind the project, whose quiet tenacity held it together;

and to the navigator of this project, Leah Rosenmeier. Without her personal commitment to creating a greater public understanding of the Mi'kmaq, this project would not have been possible.

Welcome

In 1930 and 1931, anthropologist Frederick Johnson, then 27 years old, visited seven Mi'kmaw communities–Chapel Island, Eskasoni, Merigomish Island, Millbrook, Sydney (Kings Road and Membertou) and Waycobah (Whycocomagh) in Nova Scotia and Miawpukek (Conne River) in Newfoundland–"in search of ethnological information." He listened to stories, collected materials and took about 200 photographs, which inspired the exhibition *Mikwite'lmanej Mikmaqi'k: Let Us Remember the Old Mi'kmaq.* This book captures the exhibition, and allows images not included in the exhibition to be published.

From 1997 to 1999, we, the curators, held seven community meetings to share and discuss Johnson's photographs with more than forty Elders from the communities Johnson had visited. Throughout this book, the voices and stories of these Elders and other present-day Mi'kmaw people introduce us to the lives represented in these photographs and lead us back to the early and mid-20th century and into Mi'kma'ki, the Mi'kmaw homeland. We hope you enjoy the time you spend with the people here–they continue to live with and among the Mi'kmaq and others in visible and not so visible ways.

Unless otherwise noted, these photographs were taken by anthropologist Frederick Johnson in 1930 and 1931. The Johnson photographs are in the collections of the Robert S. Peabody Museum of Archaeology, Phillips Academy, Andover, Massachusetts, and the National Museum of the American Indian, Smithsonian Institution, Washington, D.C.

1930/31 ek, Ji'nm teluisit Frederick Johnson, tewijekiss tapuiskaq jel lluikenek aqq pemkekinutmasis tan skwijinuk we'jitasni'k ki's saq, nemitukwalasni'k L'nuk wikutijik Mi'kma'ki aqq Taqamkuk. Nemitukwatkisnn lluikenek tesikl Mi'kma'ki'l. Jiksituasni'k atukwatijik L'nuk aqqpukweli wasoqitesmasni'k Mikmaqi'k. Na wejiaq wula nike ki'l jiksitmn aqq ankaptumnn sa'qoweyl wasoqitestaqnn klamann mikwite, tmatisnu iapju Mikmaqi'k.

Tim Bernard
Catherine Anne Martin
Leah Rosenmeier

Graphics derived from petroglyphs at Kejimkujik, like the one to the left, occur throughout the book.

Mi'kma'ki: The Mi'kmaw World

Pictures and stories tie people together over time and space. For many Mi'kmaq, the family members and loved ones in these photographs are still present in their everyday lives.

The images are also important because they show a time just before a series of major changes imposed by Canadian Federal and Provincial policy disrupted Mi'kmaw life in the Canadian Maritimes. Within a few years of 1930, the lives of these people were profoundly altered by relocation, residential schooling, and legal discrimination.

Mi'kmaw people lived through difficult experiences and continue to maintain a sense of their past and shared identity. Photographs like these contribute to the process of integrating the past into the present, and to building a future connected to family and centered in community. As Albert Marshall puts it, the pictures are "a trigger for stories."

Harriet (Lewis) Joe
Miawpukek (Conne River), Newfoundland, 1931

Harriet Joe is the great-grandmother of Mi'sel Joe, the current Saqamaw (Chief) at Miawpukek as
well as the daughter of Morris Lewis who was the first Nikanus (District Chief) to be appointed in 1860 by the
Kji-Saqamaw (Grand Chief).

Nannette "Janet" Abram
Millbrook, Nova Scotia, 1930

Nannette Abram's house was one of the first in the Millbrook community to enjoy an indoor hand water pump. Up to the 1930s, people got their water from outdoor wells and pumps.

Flora Jane Paul
Merigomish, Nova Scotia, 1930

Mary Brooks, an Elder living today at Indian Brook, played with Flora Jane (shown on page 82) as a young girl. Apparently, Flora Jane's parents, Peter and Mary Anne Paul, were known for being protective, just as Flora Jane was known for her independent spirit. Mary Brooks relates that she and Flora Jane would convince Mary's father to give them errands to run, providing an excuse for the girls to get outside and play.

The Mi'kmaw World

Shoreline
Eskasoni, Nova Scotia, 1930

The shoreline at Eskasoni still looks like this, although today homes line the waterfront. People recalled that Noel Jeddore, the Saqamaw (Chief) from Miawpukek, Newfoundland, lived in the tent shown beyond the road during the first years that he lived at Eskasoni.
In his memory, the road was recently renamed Noel Street.

Southwest Brook
Miawpukek, (Conne River)
  Newfoundland, 1931

Today, Southwest Brook, known locally as Sou'west Brook, is a popular swimming hole and the primary source of fresh water for the community. It looks much the same now as it did in 1931.

Wi'sik'
Waycobah (Whycocomagh),
 Nova Scotia, 1930

Johnson recorded this place as Wi'sik' in 1930, although the name didn't carry significance for people we spoke with from Waycobah or Eskasoni.

Bridge at Grand Narrows
Iona, Nova Scotia, 1930

The railway bridge at Grand Narrows was a "hell of a place to get through." Some Elders at Eskasoni thought the schooner was Peter Cremo's; it shows up in a number of Johnson's images. Peter Cremo's schooner was used to ferry people from Wagmatcook, Eskasoni, and Waycobah to the mission at Chapel Island.

The Mi'kmaw World

Hughie Googoo
Eskasoni, Nova Scotia, 1930

Hughie Googoo was a great runner who competed at marathons throughout the Atlantic Provinces, and a fine fiddler and prayer leader. He was married to Angeline (Stevens) Googoo.

Harriet Bartlett
Millbrook, Nova Scotia, 1930

Harriet Bartlett was the mother of Susan (Bartlett) Sack. She used to bring live trout to her son-in-law, Henry Sack, on Good Friday to test the pureness of his well. The fate of the fish indicated whether the water was good or bad.

Hillside
Miawpukek (Conne River), Newfoundland, 1931

Miawpukek Elders identified these homes as belonging to Paul Benoit (obscured by the trees), Andrew Joe (left center), Frank Benoit (large white house with side buildings, right center), and George Benoit (in far right foreground).

Hillside and Southwest Brook
Miawpukek (Conne River), Newfoundland, 1931

Most people at Miawpukek believed the house pictured to the right to be Uncle Matty Jeddore's, and the house pictured in the left background to be Stephen John's.

Frederick Johnson
Sept Îles, Quebec, 1927
Photographer unknown

Fred Johnson worked with Algonquian people throughout North America during his early career. From 1917 to 1931, in Innu, Cree, Annishinabe, and Mi'kmaw communities from Quebec to Newfoundland, Johnson talked with people about their lives and histories, and took hundreds of pictures. He was curator of the Robert S. Peabody Museum from 1936 to 1967 and then director until his retirement in 1969.

Frank "Jeway" Francis' house
Eskasoni, Nova Scotia, 1930

Frank "Jeway" Francis' house no longer stands at Eskasoni.

Peter Wilmot
Millbrook, Nova Scotia, 1930

Peter Wilmot was a Saqamaw (Chief) at Pictou Landing early in his life, and later on the Saqamaw at Millbrook. Some Mi'kmaq had special relationships with animals, often reflected in their ability to communicate with them. Peter is remembered as such a person and his fame as a hunter lives on today through many stories. Kenny Martin and the late Denny Gloade from the Millbrook community related one of them:

> *One day Peter went to the woods where the moose were yarding to smoke his pipe. Sitting down against a moose that was asleep, Peter lit up his pipe. As the story goes, some time later the moose woke up. "Eh, Pielo" (Oh, Peter—it's you) he said, and then promptly went back to sleep.*

Nikmatut: All my relations

"Wejisqaliey: It is a fact that we have always been part of the earth...."
Mi'kmaw chiefs, 1749

The Mi'kmaw word *Nikmatut* expresses relationships of family and community—that which is related. Many of these relationships extend to distant places. For Mi'kmaq these relationships are not just biological, but cultural and spiritual. More than anything else, Nikmatut—relationships between family and friends—define Mi'kma'ki.

Johnson photographed extended families or clans in the communities he visited. Then, as now, Mi'kmaq lived not only in the Atlantic Provinces, but throughout northeastern North America and the world. The "Boston States" and Maine are considered to be within Mi'kma'ki. These extended families and areas are shown in this chapter.

Wula kluswaqnn, "NIKMATUT" teluek na msit L'nuk akutultijik msit tami, mita nekmukk na melkiknewa'tu'tij Mi'kmawey. Wula wasoqitestaqnn nemiatisk Gouldaq aqq Morrisaq.
Itikik Mi'kmaq nemistisk elt nekmukk tan tuju siowitiayk. Sa'q wikultisni'k L'nuk wula tett mita ewikasik msit tami. Wejatikemk Kluskape'we'l atukwaqann ta'n wejitasikl wula Mi'kma'ki. L'nuk na wejisqaliatijik Kiju Maqmikowituk aqq iapju na imutitaq wula telkik wsitqamu.

Mary (Marshall) Gould
Eskasoni, Nova Scotia, 1930

Mary Gould was married to Keptin Francis Gould, and is the mother of Noel and Jane Gould. This is one of several photographs Johnson took of Mary. Traditional Mi'kmaw regalia like Mary's is worn to mark special occasions such as St. Anne's Day.

Francis "Tkalaq" Gould
Eskasoni, Nova Scotia, 1930

Francis Gould was one of the Keptins or
Captains of the Sante Mawiomi or Grand
Council. Keptins are responsible for helping
to organize the Sante Mawiomi, the
traditional Mi'kmaw governing body. Led by
the Kji-Saqamaw or Grand Chief, the
Council provides continuity and direction
for all Mi'kmaw communities.

Jane Gould (right)
 and Harriet "Alietji'j" Denny (left)
Eskasoni, Nova Scotia, 1930

Jane Gould is the daughter of Francis and
Mary Gould, and the sister of Noel. She is
standing with Harriet Denny, who was
known as Alietji'j (Little Harriet). The
Denny family was another of the large
families at Eskasoni that Johnson
photographed; other Denny family members
appear throughout the book.

All My Relations

Margaret "Maggie" (MacCleod) Gould and Mary Jane Gould
Eskasoni, Nova Scotia, 1930

Maggie was married to Simon Gould, who died sometime later. Their daughter, Mary Jane, stands in the doorway. Eventually Maggie married Thomas Battiste of Chapel Island, and they lived at Eskasoni.

Jane Gould
Eskasoni, Nova Scotia, 1930

Jane Gould, shown also on page 15 with Harriet Denny, married Noel T. Paul and had three daughters, Julia and Elizabeth, and Mary who lives in Boston, Massachusetts.

Noel Gould with eels and chickens
Eskasoni, Nova Scotia, 1930

Noel Gould was the son of Francis and Mary, and brother of Jane. Although other families kept chickens, the Goulds were known as a farming family. A traditional food, saltwater eels are still speared at night in the Bras d'Or Lake and other areas throughout the Atlantic Provinces. They are usually smoked or dried.

Noel's wife, Sonnet (Denny) was a prestigious prayer leader. They had four children, Clara, Charlie, Mali and Janie.

All My Relations

Newfoundland and the "Boston States"

Many stories about the people in these photographs tell of individuals and families moving back and forth between the Atlantic Provinces, Quebec, Maine, Massachusetts and other places; some stayed briefly and others for generations. Sometimes people moved because of hardship or tragedy, at other times simply to be with family members or to take advantage of new opportunities.

There is a long history of Mi'kmaq traveling between Newfoundland and Cape Breton in particular, but other areas of the Maritimes as well. Because of this history, there remain close ties between the Nova Scotia and Newfoundland communities. The history of Miawpukek, the community at Conne River, Newfoundland, reflects the diversity of Mi'kmaw experiences in the Atlantic Provinces. Mi'kmaq have lived in Newfoundland since time immemorial. Although recognized through Provincial and Federal agreements and by other Newfoundlanders as a Mi'kmaw community, Miawpukek was not formally acknowledged by the Federal government as a Native community with status until 1984.

1931 ek, Fred Johnson na wejiep Taqamkuk api mitukwalapnip na L'nuk wikulijik Miawpukek-Conne River. Ko'pel Nu'l na mu ketu nenuaqipnip nekmukk misoqo 1984 ek kata awnaqa aji kelu'k telalasni'k mïta nekmukk mu teli penaqotasnikipni'k saq nike itikik L'nuk. Miawpukek L'nuk alsumsisni'k tan teli asuitatij msit tami. Wula wasoqitestaqnn aqq atukwaqann telimuksikl na nekmowey.

(page 19)
Mi'kma'ki: Mi'kmaw Territory
Map by Eastern Woodland Publishing
Truro, Nova Scotia, 1999

Today there are more than 30,000 Mi'kmaq in at least 33 communities in Maine and the Atlantic Provinces. Mi'kma'ki, the Mi'kmaw aboriginal homeland, contains seven districts as shown on the map to the right.

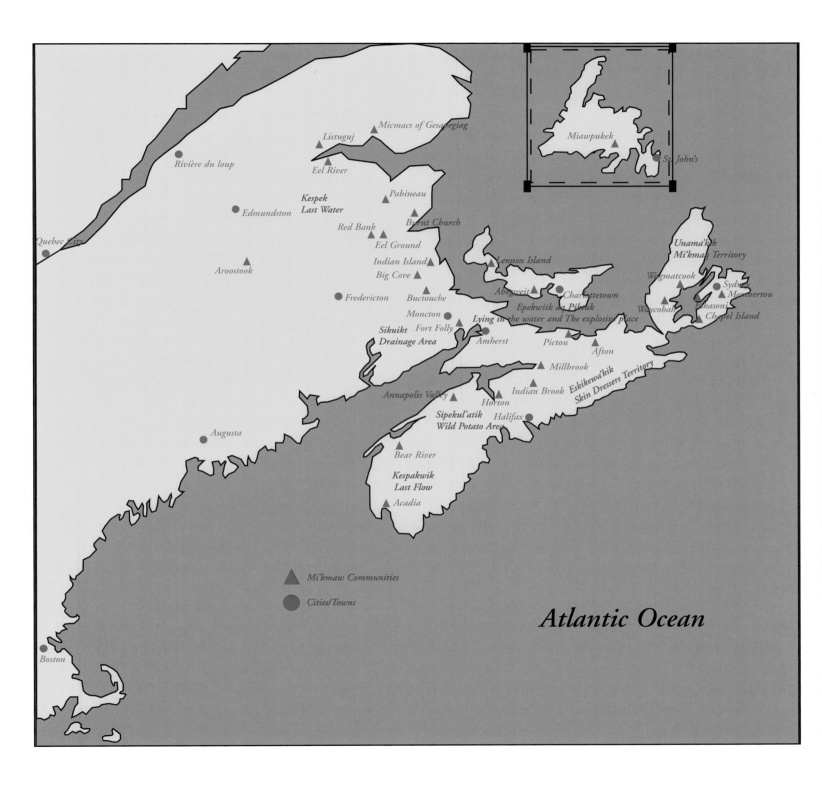

Micmacs of Gesgapegiag

Listuguj

Eel River

Pabineau

Kespek
Last Water

Rivière du loup

Edmundston

Red Bank

Burnt Church

Quebec City

Eel Ground

Aroostook

Indian Island

Big Cove

Lennox Island

Unama'kik
Mi'kmaq Territory

Fredericton

Buctouche

Abegweit

Charlottetown

Waycobah

Wagmatcook

Sydney

Membertou

Epekwitk aq Piktuk

Eskasoni

Moncton

Lying in the water and The explosive place

Chapel Island

Sikuikt
Drainage Area

Fort Folly

Amherst

Pictou

Afton

Millbrook

Eskikewa'kik
Skin Dressers Territory

Augusta

Annapolis Valley

Indian Brook

Horton

Sipekul'atik
Wild Potato Area

Halifax

Bear River

Kespakwik
Last Flow

Acadia

Miawpukek

St. John's

Boston

▲ Mi'kmaw Communities

● Cities/Towns

Atlantic Ocean

Mali Pelasi (Herney) Denny
Eskasoni, Nova Scotia, 1930

The story of Mali Pelasi Herney tells us much about the connections between communities in Maine and Nova Scotia. When her sisters Judina (Herney) Marshall and Kate (Herney) Michael drowned while traveling to sell baskets, Mali Pelasi and her husband, Michael R. Denny, moved to Maine, where two of her daughters still live.

Steven and Harriet (Lewis) Joe
Miawpukek (Conne River), Newfoundland, 1931

Steven and Harriet (Lewis) Joe were the great-grandparents of the current Saqamaw, Mi'sel Joe. In 1860 the Kji-Saqamaw (Grand Chief) in Nova Scotia appointed Harriet's father, Morris Lewis, as first Nikanus (District Chief) at Miawpukek because the territory had become too much to keep up. The Joes and Jeddores are two of the original families in Miawpukek.

All My Relations

Noel Jeddore
Eskasoni, Nova Scotia, 1930

Noel Jeddore was the Saqamaw at Miawpukek until 1921 when he left the community. The priest, Father St. Croix, gave the people a choice: either not to speak Mi'kmaq or leave the community. Faced with such an ultimatum, the Jeddores, along with the Martins, Joes, Matthews, McDonalds, and Benoits moved to Nova Scotia. When he left, Noel hung a medal in the church. Today the medal still embodies the memory of families forced to leave their community.

Mary "Ami" Jeddore
Miawpukek (Conne River), Newfoundland, 1931

Mary and Joe Jeddore, called Ami and Amité, were very important to the Miawpukek community. Ami was a medicine woman and Amité a prayer leader. Both were caregivers in traditional ways and highly regarded. Their home was one of the central places where the community steered visitors like Johnson and where priests stayed during their visits. It seems likely that Johnson stayed with them, as many of the pictures taken in Miawpukek are of the Jeddores.

All My Relations

Charlotte (Paul) Wilmot (left),
Charlie Wilmot (right)
Millbrook, Nova Scotia, 1930

People at Millbrook and Pictou Landing had much to say about "Uncle Charlie" and "Aunt Charlotte." Charlie's father, Peter, was Millbrook's founder and first Saqamaw. Charlie and Charlotte moved to Indian Brook during Centralization and then back to Millbrook during the 1940s. Madeline Martin recalls that Charlotte spent her summers with Ellie Sark at Pictou Landing.

Earlier in their lives, the Wilmots lived in Boston, traveling between Nova Scotia and Boston for seventeen years. Many Mi'kmaq have spent time in the Boston area or have family who still live there. In Nova Scotia, the northeastern U.S. is often called the "Boston States." Charlotte and Charlie's son was killed while working for the Boston subway system.

The family of Gene Winter, the current Honorary Curator at the Robert S. Peabody Museum, knew Charlie Wilmot well. Gene relates this story: "Charlie Wilmot helped to run my grandparent's farm in Tewksbury, Massachusetts, before

World War I. He and my grandmother talked about Indian and English medicines. When a doctor said my Uncle Fred's pneumonia was incurable, Charlie treated him with a skunk cabbage medicine. My grandmother's words were 'the next day he was sitting up in bed asking for something to eat!' I heard this story dozens of times.
For years, she and I collected plants, bark and roots in the woods as Charlie had taught her." Charlie also showed Gene's uncle how to trap muskrats and otters along the Shawsheen River. Gene remembers the drying boards hanging in the barn years later.

Kluskap's Cave
Waycobah (Whycocomagh), Nova Scotia, 1930

Land is a part of Nikmatut, just as family is. Although people occupied different areas throughout the year, extended families returned to the same places from generation to generation. The Kluskap stories and other tales from long ago are embedded in certain land formations, and in petroglyphs found throughout Nova Scotia that mark important places and suggest maps of the region. Kluskap is a mystical figure who appears in many Mi'kmaw legends–stories passed down from generation to generation. This picture shows Kluskap's Cave on the shores of the Bras d'Or Lake.

Where Kluskap struck the rock
Waycobah (Whycocomagh), Nova Scotia, 1930

Here "Kluskap struck the rock" in a story where he chases the beaver throughout Nova Scotia. A version of this story by Benjamin Brooks was published in 1990, translated from the original in Mi'kmaq:

They started out from Cape Breton. He [Kluskap] chased him right up to Canso where he caught sight of him. When he saw him…at Canso, he hit him there with a rock. That's where he split the mountain…in Canso. The beaver got away. They continued along up to Truro. At Truro, the beaver got in the water again at Salmon River. They went downstream…. That's where he saw him again at Five Islands. That's where he hit him again with five rocks. [There] are now five islands. Now the beaver starts out again. He goes to Partridge Island. The beaver has his dwelling at Partridge Island. That's where he chased out the beaver. The beaver got real scared, then he escaped once more. He riled up the bay then, and it has been riley ever since….It's not known where the beaver went….

A few of Johnson's pictures are of non-Native people who lived in Mi'kmaw communities in the 1930s. Ada Googoo married into the community, whereas Jimmy McKenzie was born in it. Like others over time, these people were considered part of the community.

Joe and Ada Googoo
Eskasoni, Nova Scotia, 1930

Ada Googoo, who was from Baddeck, Nova Scotia, was not Mi'kmaq. She died at an early age and they never had children. Joe later married Nancy Gabriel, and they had a daughter, Mary, who still lives at Eskasoni.

Jimmy McKenzie returning from Merigomish Island
Merigomish, Nova Scotia, 1930

Elder Mary Brooks recalls that Jimmy's mother, who was not Mi'kmaq, came to Pictou pregnant with Jimmy. There he was born and raised, and lived out his life. She recalls Jimmy's strong commitment to the Pictou Landing community and his reluctance to live and interact with non-Mi'kmaq.

Jimmy McKenzie at a camp site
Merigomish, Nova Scotia, 1930

Jimmy's children live on today in a number of Mi'kmaw communities. Elders relate that non-Native children were accepted and cared for by the community.

All My Relations

Stephen and Isabel (Poulette) Morris and family
Waycobah (Whycocomagh), Nova Scotia, 1930

In Waycobah Fred Johnson stayed with Stephen and Isabel Morris, who are pictured here. Left to right in the back row are: Annie Claire (Morris) Googoo, Mary Bridget (Morris) Paul, Nancy (Sylliboy) Morris, Leo Morris, Matthew Morris, Edward Morris, and Levi Poulette. Stephen and Isabel (Poulette) Morris sit in the front row with Mary Bridget's children between them. Stephen and Chris Morris, pictured to the right, were brothers.

**Chris Morris, Peter Paul, Mali A'n Morris, and Mary Josephine (MacCleod) Morris
Eskasoni, Nova Scotia, 1930**

Johnson wrote later that at Eskasoni and Waycobah, "there were four old people with whom I became very friendly. They knew me as 'son' and I replied with 'grandmother' and 'grandfather'." We suspect that these four old people are Chris and Mary Josephine Morris, and Stephen and Isabel Morris. He was not the first anthropologist to visit with the Morrises. Clara Dennis and Elsie Clews Parsons, among others, had visited with them in previous years.

Ann Madeline "Nanaoqji'j" Poulette
Waycobah (Whycocomagh), Nova Scotia,
1930

Ann Madeline Poulette was the mother of
Isabel Morris and Levi Poulette. People at
Eskasoni told us that in the 1930s wigwams
were often used as workshops and places
where people spent time during the day.
Mrs. Poulette made baskets in this wigwam,
located behind Stephen Morris' house.

Stephen Morris
Waycobah (Whycocomagh), Nova Scotia,
1930

Stephen Morris was the father of Annie
Claire (Morris) Googoo, who remembers
hosting Johnson when he stayed at their
house in Waycobah.

Matthew Morris
Eskasoni, Nova Scotia, 1930

Matthew Morris was the son of Chris and Mary Josephine Morris, and the brother of Mali A'n and Stephen Morris. He was visiting his uncle, aunt and cousins on the day that Johnson took the picture of Stephen and Isabel Morris' family. He is standing in the back row of the group on page 30. There was a fair amount of coming and going between the communities.

Annie Claire (Morris) Googoo
Eskasoni, Nova Scotia, 1999
Photograph by Catherine Martin

Annie Claire (Morris) Googoo is the daughter of Stephen (shown to the left) and Isabel Morris. She was 11 years old when Johnson stayed with her family at Waycobah. She remembers him as a quiet and unobtrusive man, "who just wanted to hear the stories from the old people."

She stands in a white dress to the far left in the picture of her family on page 30.

All My Relations

Stephen Morris
Eskasoni, Nova Scotia, 1930

Stephen Morris was the son of Chris and Mary Josephine Morris and brother to Mali A'n and Matthew. Stephen was killed in an accident while he was working on a wood pulp boat.

Chris and Mary Josephine Morris playing
  waltes
Eskasoni, Nova Scotia, 1930

Chris and Mary Josephine had six children, Peter, Charlie, Mali A'n, Stephen, Noel and Matthew.

Here, Chris and Mary Josephine are playing waltes, a traditional Mi'kmaw game. Mi'kmaw people wore regalia, played waltes, and used wigwams at certain times of the year and for various activities. There are, however, a number of images that look as if Johnson staged them—this is one.

Mali A'n (Morris) Sylliboy
Eskasoni, Nova Scotia, 1930

Mali A'n was the daughter of Chris and
Mary Josephine Morris and sister of Matthew
and Stephen Morris. She married Frank
Sylliboy; their daughter, Marion (Sylliboy)
Paul is an educator.

Nancy (Sylliboy) Morris
Eskasoni, Nova Scotia, 1999
Photograph by Catherine Martin

Nancy (Sylliboy) Morris was married to
Edward Morris, the son of Stephen and
Isabel Morris.

She is the great-aunt of exhibition curators
Catherine Martin and Tim Bernard.

Nancy recalls 1930 as a time of self-
sufficiency and independence. Among many
other ventures later in her life, Nancy
operated one of the few ambulances serving
Mi'kmaw people in Cape Breton.

Harriet (Joe) Denny (left and right)
Eskasoni, Nova Scotia, 1930

Harriet Denny was the wife of Simon Denny,
one of the Keptins of the Grand Council.

Denny family area
Eskasoni, Nova Scotia, 1930

As well as photographing individuals and
families, Johnson took pictures of the places
within communities where members of
extended families lived over generations.
Until the late 19th century, many Mi'kmaw
families traveled to different areas in Nova
Scotia, and typically returned to the same
places from year to year. As reserves became
established, certain areas became associated
with particular families. Through age-old
associations with families and stories, land is
integral to communities for more than the
materials and natural resources it provides.

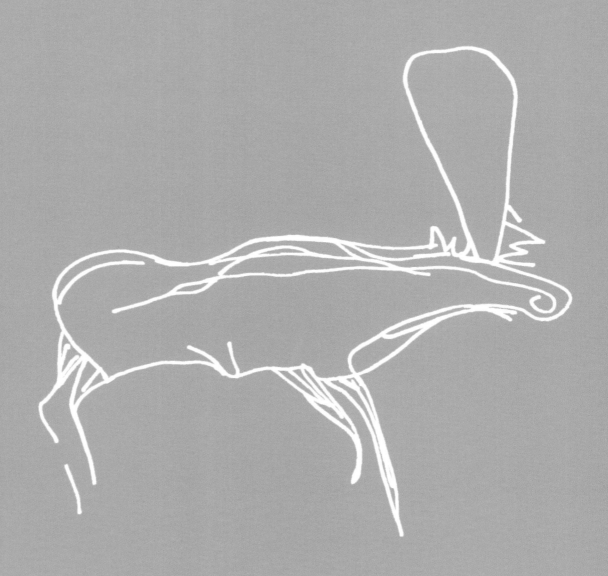

Netukulimk: Living in the land

*"People are always saying that Native people survived—
No, I don't buy that. Oh, we did more than just survive,
my dear child—we lived."*
Sarah Francis

Mi'kmaq today remember the early 20th century as a time of independence. Elders do not recall feeling poor, and do not recall widespread hunger, sickness or confinement, all of which were more common in later experiences. Natural resources were available to sustain local economies, and people knew how to make use of them. This self-sufficiency was key to the security people felt in their lives.

Ki's saq, L'nukik na mawi weljaqo'ltipni'k aqq mu elita'suwala'tika wena. Keluksipnek aqq tajiko'tipni'k na tan teloltijik na tujuw. Nata maliamsutipni'k aqq wejiaqsip mimajuaqanmuow maqmikewiktuk aqq sitmuk.

Helen (Sylliboy) Denny with wooden flowers
Eskasoni, Nova Scotia, 1930

Helen was the wife of Peter Denny and mother of Harriet, Noel, Joe, Semisel, Sonnet, Annie, Jane and Helen. She is holding flowers most likely made of maple splints. Helen, and Harriet "Alietji'j" Denny and Susie (Denny) Marshall who are shown on pages 42 and 43, make three generations of skilled basket makers.

**Peter "Pie'l Po'l" with, his son, Peter "JiJi" Denny, on his work horse (*te'sipowji'j*) splitting ash
Eskasoni, Nova Scotia, 1930**

Peter may be splitting maple for his wife Helen's wooden flowers, or perhaps ash for baskets. Ash, both white and black, is the wood of choice for baskets because it splits naturally into smooth splints that make strong and beautiful final products. Maple can be split into very narrow widths and twisted into various forms without breaking.

Living in the Land

Harriet Denny "Alietji'j" making baskets
Eskasoni, Nova Scotia, 1930

Along with being a wonderful basket maker, Harriet, also shown on page 15, was a prayer leader in the community and someone that people "went to for advice." As a young girl she fell from a tree and broke her back, but people assured us that she was "as healthy as a bug." Harriet's daughter, Susie, shown to the right, carries on her mother's and grandmother's skills as a basket maker.

Susan (Denny) Marshall making a basket
Eskasoni, Nova Scotia, 1997
Photograph by Clayton Paul

Susie is the daughter of Harriet and granddaughter of Peter and Helen Denny. She is well known for her beautifully made baskets.

Living in the Land

Joe "Amité" Jeddore tanning skin
Miawpukek (Conne River), Newfoundland, 1931

Along with showing Fred Johnson how to catch and smoke salmon and make a bundle (shown on pages 112-115), Joe Jeddore showed him how to tan skins. Joe is most likely cleaning caribou skin with a scraper made from a caribou leg bone, a tool still used today.

John Herney with ash splints
Eskasoni, Nova Scotia, 1930

John Herney was the father of Judina, Kate and Mali Pelasi Herney.

He carries ash splints used for a variety of purposes, including baskets and wooden flowers. Both men and women made baskets, and were involved in harvesting the ash, pounding the logs to make splints, and weaving the final product.

Camp
Miawpukek (Conne River),
Newfoundland, 1931

Camps like these were used after European contact for hunting, fishing, and gathering other resources.

Living in the Land

Joe Jeddore cleaning salmon
Miawpukek (Conne River), Newfoundland, 1931

Joe and Mary Jeddore were very important to the Miawpukek community. This is one of a series of images taken by Fred Johnson as Joe Jeddore showed him how to catch and smoke a salmon. The full series appears on pages 112-113. Salmon are still plentiful in Newfoundland, where sportsmen come from around the world to fish.

"Seems to me that Indians weren't that poor. How could we be so happy if we were poor? Because we were happy....we were always celebrating."
Mary Brooks

Chris Morris with eels
Eskasoni, Nova Scotia, 1930

Chris Morris posed with his eel rack in front of the wigwam that he and his wife, Mary Josephine, had just finished making.

As Johnson's photographs show, in 1930 most livelihoods still came directly from the land. Hunting, fishing, farming, and making tools and other goods from wood still locally available, were central to community economies.

In Nova Scotia in 1906, Mi'kmaw people moved among more than 43 areas at different times of the year, for fishing in the spring and summer, and hunting in the fall. Many people today remember older generations not living on reserves, but in their own communities and moving freely through the land.

Ki's saq, na L'nuk majukwalapnn tan telasitl tepkunasetl, mita wejiaqip minajuaqanm natel. Ewikasik 1906ek, Na Mi'kmaq ajitasnik ne'wis kaq jel si'st te's newtiwipunqek Mi'kma'ki. Alsutmi'ti's tan tett eltajik - si'wk, nipk, toqa'k aqq kesik. 1930ek wula wasoqitestaqnn teluwekl L'nukik na me' nata netukultisni'k aqq wel mimajultisni'k tan tett wikultipni'k.

(pages 48 and 49)

**Noel Lewis at hunting camp
Miawpukek (Conne River),
  Newfoundland, 1931**

Here, Noel Lewis sits in a
hunting camp. He was
remembered as the "mailman"
because he was the one who
traveled back and forth between
Miawpukek and Cape Breton
with news and messages. As in
many communities, people are
still the best way for important
news to travel.

**Louise Mali A'n (Denny)
  Morris and Rita Morris
Eskasoni, Nova Scotia, 1930**

Louise was known for her fine
shopping baskets, usually made
out of maple splints and dyed
with an eosine dye. Since Louise
is dressed in regalia and has a
large bag of baskets with her, it is
likely that Johnson took her
picture as she was on her way to
sell her baskets. Louise Morris'
daughter Rita stands behind her.
As an adult, Rita moved to
Boston, Massachusetts.

Poqjulsultimkek: The Move

"Up until centralization, which was in the early 40s, Native people hunted and fished anywhere and went everywhere, and nobody bothered you..."
Ben Martin

By 1930, two trends in Federal government policies towards Native people had profound impact on Mi'kmaw communities: increasing pressure to relocate Mi'kmaw people, and the imposition of a residential school. Efforts to concentrate Native people into designated areas began about 1780, with Indian land areas established throughout the late-18th and 19th centuries. In 1876, the Canadian government passed the Indian Act, which determines the system of government control of reserve activities. A number of revisions and amendments have been passed since the original legislation, and in 1952 all policies and related legislation were subsumed under the Indian Act. In the early 20th century, through the Indian Act and other formal and informal policies, Indian agents and other government officials became increasingly aggressive about relocating Mi'kmaw communities. One of the most aggressive relocation efforts occurred in Sydney, where the Mi'kmaw community at Kings Road was moved out of the downtown area to Membertou.

1876ek, Ka'plnu'l na kisitoqsisp wikatiknn teluisik Indian Act. Ketu szkzpalapmi' L'nuk aqq menuaqalpnik atlasiewitasultinow. Pukwelki'k L'nuk poqjiwsultipni'k aqq winijanuaqi'k ela'la'tisnik nuji kinamatmuo'koml teluiskl "Residential Schools." Indian Act na pukweli opala'la'jik na L'nuk aqq me ketu alsuma'ji pasik L'nuk na me matnmi'tij aqq pemi swis'ka'tu'tij nekmowey.

Kings Road reserve, Nova Scotia, ca. 1910
National Archives of Canada, PA-082488

The Kings Road reserve was located along Kings Road in Sydney until 1928. An amendment to the Indian Act in 1911 allowed the government to relocate Native communities adjacent to non-Native communities with more than 8,000 people. Under this provision in 1916, a judge ruled that the Mi'kmaw community at Kings Road should be relocated. By 1928 all but two of the Mi'kmaw families were removed to the newly-built Membertou reserve, shown to the right.

Membertou, Nova Scotia, 1930

The Kings Road reserve property was considered valuable because of its proximity to downtown Sydney. The community experienced constant pressure from the late 19th century onward to transfer its property to the government. The court case that forced the relocation stated that "without hesitation [the] removal of the Indians from the reserve was obviously in the interest of the public." Membertou was one of the first communities built by the Department of Indian Affairs expressly for the relocation of Mi'kmaw people.

Teresa (Bernard) Googoo
Sydney, Nova Scotia, 1930

Teresa (Bernard) Googoo was married to
Peter Googoo. They lived at Membertou in
1930, and probably came from the Kings
Road reserve.

In 1942, efforts to separate Native and non-Native people resulted in a formal policy known as Centralization, which proposed to remove all Mi'kmaw communities in Nova Scotia to two reserves, at Eskasoni and Shubenacadie, now called Indian Brook. Indian agents promised new homes, farming equipment and other resources if families were willing to relocate. Most of these promises were not kept.

Between 1930 and 1950, Mi'kmaq found their livelihoods increasingly restricted as access to traditional hunting and fishing areas became limited. Coupled with this restriction on movement were efforts to shape Mi'kmaw behavior. A 1927 amendment to the Indian Act outlawed many religious and economic activities of Native people throughout Canada. Priests and federal police living in Native communities confiscated traditional games such as waltes and wapnaqnk, and ceremonial objects such as pipes. In Nova Scotia, laws forbidding Native people to enter poolhalls and liquor stores were more strictly enforced than other prohibitions. Murdena Marshall remembers the story of the last raid for traditional games in Eskasoni. In February 1955 people were gathered to play waltes and other games, tell stories and feast, when the agent came in and confiscated the games; each person in the house was fined $13.50.

Stephen Googoo, Annie Christmas, Juliette Christmas, Mary Susan Marshall and Cecilia Christmas
Membertou, Nova Scotia, 1930

In 1999 Bernie Francis, a Mi'kmaw linguist, refused to pay his taxes in protest and remembrance of the Kings Road relocation. On March 22, 1999, David Muise, Cape Breton Regional Mayor, responded by apologizing to the "40 direct descendants" of those people who had been forced to move to Membertou, among whom were the descendants of the Googoos, Bernards and Christmases.

1942ek, Ka'plnu'l na me weji alsumasni L'nuk. Menuaqlapni'k mawita'new aqq poqjulsultinew klaman me atlasie'wk ki's wikultitaq ta'n tett menuweketijtelki'k Mi'kma'ki. Pukweli kespukwalasni'k L'nuk aqq weji naqitpalasni'k. Liwsultinow tapukl l'nuekatil teluisikl Eskasoni aqq Sepeknakati. Telimapni'k keluk mimajuaqnn nemitaq aqq weltekl wenjikomal wikultitaq. Eykik eltapni'k aqq eykik mu jiksitmutipni'k mita Ka'plnu'l na tapui siskwit aqq netawi ewlet.

1930 aqq 1950 ek, Patelia'sk aqq policemenaq etli alsusultipni'k wula L'nuekati'l. Apijotu'atipni'k L'nuk waltesl aqq wapnaqnk.

The Move

Janet (Gould) Marshall
Sydney, Nova Scotia, 1930

Janet Marshall was from Membertou and was married to John Marshall. They were among those who were relocated to the new Membertou reserve.

Loaded cart
Eskasoni, Nova Scotia, 1930

Although images of people actually moving their belongings during Centralization are not known, we imagine that this cart, loaded with materials to make a wigwam, looks much as it would have to transport households and belongings during the following decade.

Ultimately efforts to centralize Mi'kmaw people failed, primarily due to their resistance. Some people stayed at Eskasoni or Shubenacadie, which remain the largest Mi'kmaw communities in Nova Scotia today, but others returned to their original communities and worked to rebuild their homes.

Twentieth-century Federal Indian policy was contradictory. There was an effort to assimilate Mi'kmaq culturally, yet government policy and action continued to separate Native and non-Native communities geographically. If people chose to assert their Mi'kmaw identity, they were subject to increased discrimination. Prior to 1952 when all policies and related legislation were consolidated under the Indian Act, assimilation was possible through the Enfranchisement Act, which in conjunction with the Indian Act and other related legislation, granted citizenship to Mi'kmaq only if they gave up their status as Indians.

Many Mi'kmaq today carry the knowledge of broken promises and the hardships that past generations lived through. They acknowledge how much has changed—how life was restricted by the loss of access to the land and by the prejudice their communities and families faced.

Michael Henry Sack
Millbrook, Nova Scotia, 1930

Michael and Susan Sack moved to Shubenacadie during Centralization, and like many people from Millbrook stayed for only a few years before returning to rebuild the community.

Unlike some Mi'kmaw communities that were not close to urban areas like Truro, Millbrook was close to markets, transportation and opportunities for wage labor. At the time of Centralization there were 43 families living at Millbrook and

Susan (Bartlett) Sack
Millbrook, Nova Scotia, 1930

about half the adults were employed in the town of Truro. These circumstances led to few people leaving Millbrook during Centralization. Of those that did, like the Sacks, most returned soon after leaving.

The Move

"Shubie School": The Shubenacadie Residential School

"It must be awful, when you can't open your mouth or talk to anybody next to you. I walked into the little girls' recreation room....their mouths were taped ...medicine tape...the heavy stuff you know.... I bet some of them don't even remember that because they were so used to being treated like that."
Mary Brooks

Unlike Centralization, which was policy only in Nova Scotia, the Shubenacadie Residential School that opened in 1930 was intended for Native children throughout the Canadian Maritimes. The school was seen as a key mechanism for assimilation. Children who–according to the Indian agent–did not have "proper care" or were "in trouble" at school were sent to Shubenacadie. When Shubenacadie closed in 1967, more than a thousand children had passed through its doors.

For many children, life at "Shubie" was damaging physically and emotionally. Children were not allowed to speak Mi'kmaq, their own language, and were punished harshly for breaking rules. The "curriculum" consisted primarily of religious teachings and manual labor. For some Mi'kmaq, however, the residential experience was not painful, and has remained important into their adult lives.

Repeated attempts by family members to get their children back failed. People remember Indian agents promising that children would be returned if families agreed to relocate to one of the centralized reserves at Eskasoni or Shubenacadie.

Shubenacadie Residential School
Shubenacadie, Nova Scotia
Reproduced by permission from Russell Robinson

"Shubie School" accommodated children of all ages. This austere building stands in stark contrast to the small day schools in communities, and certainly to the homes children were used to.

Father Brown with children
Shubenacadie Residential School, Shubenacadie, Nova Scotia
Courtesy of the Archives of the Sisters of Charity, Halifax, Nova Scotia

Father Brown with the children at Shubenacadie in the mid-1940s. The teaching sisters stand at the rear.

William, Madeline (Abram) and Richard Sylliboy
Millbrook, Nova Scotia, 1930

Although the Shubenacadie Residential School was damaging for many children, life in the communities was not immune to hardship. Richard Sylliboy, the boy in this picture, probably about five years of age, died several years later of tuberculosis. This was just about the time that Centralization was formally implemented.

Margaret (Prosper) Stevens holds daughter Bridget with son Daniel at her side
Chapel Island, Nova Scotia, 1930

Neither Daniel nor Bridget went to Shubenacadie, which reflects the fact that not all Mi'kmaw children went to the Shubie School. It wasn't always clear to children who stayed home whether going to Shubie was a good thing. Some older people today recall other children returning from Shubie in new shoes and clothes. Despite these provisions life at Shubie remains shrouded in silence for many adults today, being too painful to share with family and friends.

Boys pitching pennies
Eskasoni, Nova Scotia, 1930

"Pitch" was a common game in Mi'kmaw communities at this time. These boys were remembered, from left to right, as Noel "Wai" Michael, Stephen Marshall, John Marshall, Martin Dennis, Frank Dennis, and Peter Paul. Noel Michael was Kate (Herney) Michael's son, and Mali Pelasi (Herney) Denny's nephew. He was sent to Shubie after his mother drowned.

"Children can't learn to be Mi'kmaq from books—you have to feel it."
Murdena Marshall

Mary "Maemay" Paul cutting bread
Shubenacadie Residential School,
  Shubenacadie, Nova Scotia
From *Out of the Depths: The Experiences*
  of Mi'kmaw Children at the Indian
  Residential School at Shubenacadie, Nova
  ***Scotia* by Isabelle Knockwood with**
  Gillian Thomas, 1992
Reproduced by permission

As in nearly all Indian residential schools in
Canada and the United States, Native
children did much of the day labor that kept
the schools going. Here, Maemay Paul cuts
bread for one of the meals.

While individual children were affected, more recently people assess the impact of the residential
school at a cultural and community level. People see the disconnection of children from their
families and communities as the most damaging effect of the "Shubie School" era. Children grew up
outside their community and away from the extended families that had raised them.

Ta'n teli wuli sku'tasik(i)p Shubie School mimajuinu'k elkimatipni wnijanua. Telta'sultipnik wuli
kina'masultitaq. Mijua'ji'jk ta'ni'k stnaqnk kisna wunki'ku ksnukewinu'k e'jntaq nekmowk elo'la'tipni. Mu
kejitasinuk(i)p eyki'k mijua'ji'jki'k ewlo'tasultitki'k. Elukojik aqq mu kekina'muajik. Atel na kejikaw
muska'sik ta'n tetuji emekotasultisni'k eyki'k mijua'ji'ki'k.

Melkiknewa'ltimk: Gaining Strength, Renewing Community

For several decades after Fred Johnson's visits, during the height of Centralization and attendance at the Shubie School, Mi'kmaw identity and ways of life were disparaged. Although the age-old relationships people shared with each other and with the land were disrupted by harsh policies and discrimination, Mi'kmaw people persisted through these changes. Johnson's photographs document important people and cultural practices that the Mi'kmaq relied on during this time.

Resistance was obvious within Mi'kmaw communities throughout this period. Although later exonerated, in 1929 Kji-Saqamaw Gabriel Sylliboy was convicted under The Lands and Forest Act for having fifteen muskrat pelts. He argued that as a Mi'kmaq, he was exempt from this Provincial legislation due to rights protected by treaties. After his conviction, hunting and fishing continued, but people kept these activities out of the public eye. Gabriel Sylliboy, Ben Christmas, Joe Julien and others worked against Centralization as well, sending letters to officials in Ottawa and protesting in other ways. In 1947 and 1948, a government commission met to talk with people about Centralization. Eventually through these efforts Centralization was curtailed. It wasn't until 1985 that Mi'kmaw hunting and fishing rights were reaffirmed.

During the time when the Mi'kmaq were under increased scrutiny and legal prohibitions, island retreats provided security and allowed people to relax with friends and family. This chapter highlights some Mi'kmaw leaders from different communities and contains a series of photographs of the annual celebration of St. Anne's Day at Merigomish Island and Chapel Island.

**Gabriel Sylliboy speaking at St. Anne's Day
Chapel Island, Nova Scotia, 1930**

Gabriel Sylliboy was the Kji-Saqamaw (Grand Chief) for all Mi'kmaq between 1918 and 1963, and was one of the great leaders of the 20th century. Gabriel was born in 1874 in Waycobah (Whycocomagh) and moved to Eskasoni later in his life. His political activities were important in securing Mi'kmaw rights in the later 20th century. Great warmth and appreciation were apparent in people's memories of Gabriel.

Peter Paul
Merigomish, Nova Scotia, 1930

Peter Paul was the husband of Mary Anne Paul, and father of Flora Jane.

Gaining Strength, Renewing Community

Joe "Amité" Jeddore (left) and Matt Burke
Miawpukek (Conne River), Newfoundland, 1931

Joe Jeddore was the brother of Noel Jeddore and, as noted, one of the important leaders in the community who helped carry people through difficult times. People gathered at the Jeddore's home to be together and share information in times of celebration and stress.

Tom Gloade
Merigomish Island,
 Nova Scotia, 1930

At the time of this picture Tom Gloade was 57 years old and living at Millbrook, where he was a mason. Tom was originally from East Mines, where a number of Millbrook families had come from after the reserve was established in 1886. In 1891, he married Mary Gloade. They were the parents of Annie Gloade.

Gaining Strength, Renewing Community

**Peter Wilmot (left and right)
Millbrook, Nova Scotia, 1930**

Peter Wilmot was a Saqamaw at Pictou Landing early in his life. After relocating to Truro, Peter negotiated with the Indian agent for land that became the Millbrook Native Community in 1886, where he was the first Saqamaw. Records indicate that he lived to be at least 106 years old; he is probably 104 in these pictures.

The founding of Millbrook is remembered by many in the community. Don Julien recorded the stories about the founding from Gerald and Charles Gloade, among others. At the turn of the 19th century, Mi'kmaq were living along the Salmon River that runs between Truro and Bible Hill. In the early fall of 1879, Peter Wilmot was hunting in the area that is now Millbrook, when he came across a bear and shot it.

While carrying the bear out of the woods he saw quite a lot of ash growing and so he asked the Indian Agent to exchange the area where Mi'kmaq were living at Christmas Crossing, now

known as King St. Crosssing. The Mi'kmaw families from Truro moved to the newly-acquired 35 acres in 1886 and started clearing their own little properties in what is today the Millbrook reserve. Additional acreage was added to the reserve in 1917 after the Halifax explosion, and again in 1954 and 1966.

Summer retreats often lasting for a week or ten days, are important as times of Melkiknewa'ltimk, when people renew ties to one another and reaffirm their sense of community. Gatherings, called Mawiomi in Mi'kmaq, have always been a part of Mi'kmaw life.

At Merigomish and Chapel Island, the last weekend in July is the time for the Procession of St. Anne, a Catholic ceremony honoring the patron saint of the Mi'kmaq. The Procession is one of many events at these retreats, where there are both visible and invisible activities—religious, political, and social. This is when the Sante Mawiomi, or Grand Council, meets. At night there is dancing, and during the day people visit and play games. Gathering together, sharing stories and food, and lots of laughter, are basic to this renewal and celebration, which continue to this day.

Mi'kmaq kesatmi'tij mawita'mk. Mawaknutma'timk aqq mawat'awultimk. Ta'n tijiw eltamk mnikuk wjit Se'ta'newimk welteskajik kitapk ta'n mna'q nemiawjik ki's sa'q. Wula tet eymn kisi Mi'kmawin keskmna'q e'jentaq aqq mawntiaq to'qomajaiaskik. Apaja'tu'n ta'n teloti'k(i)p keskmna'q pekisinukek game'kewa'j. Mijua'ji'jk kekina'mu'kik ta'n wen telwulo'tasij mi'kmawiktuk.

Going to Merigomish Island
Merigomish, Nova Scotia, 1930

Prior to 1864 the annual St. Anne mission was held at Merigomish as well as at Chapel Island and people would often attend both. The two islands are central to Mi'kmaq cultural rejuvenation and today continue to be favorite summer gathering places.

These women are heading east towards Merigomish, probably for St. Anne's day celebrations.

Traveling to Chapel Island
Bras d'Or Lake, Nova Scotia, 1930

Traveling across the Bras d'Or Lake was common, sometimes by canoe and other times in sailing boats like this one. These people in their dress clothes appear ready to celebrate.

Sante Mawiomi wigwams at Chapel Island
Chapel Island, Nova Scotia, 1930

The Sante Mawiomi (Grand Council) still meets every year at Chapel Island. The flagpole in the center right marks the Kji-Saqamaw wigwam. Wigwams from each community are clustered together.

Checker game
Chapel Island, Nova Scotia, 1930

Chapel Island was a place for people to relax. People played with "the greatest of ease and with great vigor." Along with checkers, people played cards, waltes, wapnaqnk and other games.

Gaining Strength, Renewing Community

Dance ring
Chapel Island, Nova Scotia, 1930

Murdena Marshall explains that the dance is called Neskawemk, which is a dance to thank the spirit of the animal for giving its life for food. In the dance, one displays hunting abilities and skills through a reenactment of the hunt. People sing and share stories as the dance is performed.

Peter Cremo
Chapel Island, Nova Scotia, 1930

Peter Cremo was remembered as a fisherman and prayer leader. Johnson mentions spending time with Pielo Cremeau. He was the grandfather of the late Lee Cremo (1939-1999), world-renowned fiddler who was dubbed The Golden Arm.

Flora Jane Paul, Peter Paul, Mary Paul and Tom Gloade
Merigomish Island, Nova Scotia, 1930

While many of Johnson's pictures are of Chapel Island, Mi'kmaq also gather at Merigomish Island and celebrate St. Anne's Day there. Peter and Flora Jane's regalia was probably commissioned by the Prince of Wales in 1860 for a visit he made to the Province, modeled from the Nova Scotia Coat of Arms. The image of the Native person that appears on the Nova Scotia Coat of Arms was based on drawings of Native people in Brazil.[1]

Mary Anne Paul
Merigomish, Nova Scotia, 1930

Mary Anne Paul was married to Peter Paul, and the mother of Flora Jane.

Johnson photographed the entire procession of St. Anne, including Kji-Saqamaw Gabriel Sylliboy and Father Pacifique speaking to the people. The photographs of the procession are shown in the following 7 pages. It includes the formal procession out of the church, Kji-Saqamaw Gabriel Sylliboy and then Father Pacifique giving speeches, and the formal procession back into the church. After the procession, a cannon was fired.

Processing out of the Chapel (left and above)
Chapel Island, Nova Scotia, 1930

These pictures show people processing out of the Chapel at the start of the celebration. St. Anne, known as the grandmother, is carried in her chair, *wkutputim*, with the leaders, including the Saqamaq and Keptins, and priests at the head of the line. Young girls receiving their first communion accompany the grandmother on either side.

Gabriel Sylliboy
Chapel Island, Nova Scotia, 1930

Gabriel Sylliboy led much of the St. Anne celebration and gave a speech along with prayers to the people who assembled. His duties as Kji-Saqamaw continued later with the selection of the Keptins and other political positions filled every year at Chapel Island.

Father Pacifique
Chapel Island, Nova Scotia, 1930

Father Pacifique de Valigny served the Listuguj (Restigouche) community in Quebec for over 40 years. He died there in 1943. Throughout his life, he translated the gospels and other religious works into Mi'kmaq, and worked on an orthography.

Kneeling at the cross
Chapel Island, Nova Scotia, 1930

This image does not show the people kneeling at the cross below the bushes, which Johnson's caption indicates. Kneeling at the cross was a central part of the St. Anne's observance.

Gaining Strength, Renewing Community

Returning back to the chapel (left and below)
Chapel Island, Nova Scotia, 1930

These images show the procession back to the chapel. After the procession, activities continue inside the church where people kiss the relic of St. Anne and the Grand Chief's medal. With the grandmother inside, people go outside again and pray for the sick and then process, in those days on their knees, back inside to the Saint.

Firing the cannon (left and below)
Chapel Island, Nova Scotia, 1930

Murdena Marshall explains that the cannon came from the Louisbourg area. It was originally fired as a salute when the missionaries arrived, but hasn't been used that way for a long time. More recently, young men test their strength by lifting the cannon, first to their knees, then to their chest, then to their shoulders and finally above their head. At one point a young man was over-zealous and carried it to the wharf and threw it in the water. Jean Doucette of Chapel Island had it retrieved in the early 1970s, but the carriage was never found.

Gaining Strength, Renewing Community

Wedding
Chapel Island, Nova Scotia, 1930

Weddings occurred every year at Chapel Island when a visiting priest, usually serving much of the Maritimes, was available to bless couples. These unions were blessed, but not recorded. There was no written confirmation available nor were marriage licenses issued. Baptisms, naming ceremonies and sometimes weddings still occur at Chapel Island.

Frederick Johnson's Work

"Everybody trusted him because he was an easy-going guy."
Annie Claire Googoo

Like many anthropologists of his time, Frederick Johnson was most interested in what he saw as the older, traditional aspects of Mi'kmaw life, but he also documented everyday activities. He was remembered warmly by Annie Claire (Morris) Googoo, who was 11 years old in 1930, as a quiet and unobtrusive visitor who "just wanted to hear the stories from the old people."

Johnson's experiences in Nova Scotia and Newfoundland were important ones for him. The close relationship between these visits and his understandings of the past are revealed in Johnson's subsequent work. Eight years later, as curator of the Robert S. Peabody Museum, he included activities he had learned in Mi'kmaw communities in a model village of "Woodland" Indians, set in 1500 A.D. This diorama reflects aspects of Mi'kmaw life that Johnson recorded during his visits: the Morris' baskets, eel rack, and wigwam are the most obvious.

Wula wasoqɫestaqnn kisi wsua'toql Pustunkewa'j teluisit Frederick Johnson. Ala'sisnaq Mi'kma'ki ke'skmna'q majulsultimkek aqq kesmnaq ta'puewey matntimk. Etuk mu nekm kpisinuk mu kisi apajapasulti'kɨpn kniskamijinaq eymu'ti'titek. Pikwelk ankita'suaqn wejiaq wula ankatmn wasoqtestaqnn. Eyk wen muiatk nemiaj wikma ta'n mna'q nemiaqsɨpni pasɨk nutmaji. Nike wjit e'tasiw Mi'kmaw etek wula wi'katikn ta'n kisi ankamata kniskamjijinaq.

**Mali A'n (Morris) Sylliboy (left) and Mary Josephine (MacCleod) Morris
Eskasoni, Nova Scotia, 1930**

Mary Josephine and Mali A'n stand in front of the wigwam that Mary Josephine and Chris Morris made during Johnson's visit. Johnson took a number of detailed photographs of people's regalia. Although some people think the caps show European influence, Johnson rejected this idea. He noted that they were similar to those worn by other northeastern Native groups and that they easily could have evolved from the use of a hood common in earlier times.

> "There were four old people with whom I became very friendly. They knew me as 'son' and I replied with 'grandmother' or 'grandfather'...."
> Frederick Johnson, 1943

Frederick Johnson
Mt. Washington, New Hampshire, 1924
Photographer unknown

Unfortunately, field notes from Johnson's visits to Nova Scotia and Newfoundland in 1930 and 1931 have not been located. It seems likely they were destroyed in a fire in 1981. During his visits, Johnson collected clothing, baskets, games and other materials. Notes on the inventory of these materials provide us a glimpse into some of his thoughts and opinions.

Johnson's photographs reflect an anthropological agenda that was most interested in reconstructing the past. Unlike many popular images of Native people taken during the early 20th century, however, Johnson's pictures are seen by many Mi'kmaw people today as capturing a true spirit of their communities.

In 1930-31, Johnson visited seven communities: Chapel Island, Eskasoni, Merigomish Island, Miawpukek (Conne River), Millbrook, Sydney (Membertou, Kings Road), and Waycobah (Whycocomagh). Today these and more than 26 other Mi'kmaw communities continue to change and to grow.

Frederick Johnson's Work

Susan (Bartlett) Sack
Millbrook, Nova Scotia, 1930

People at Millbrook really liked these daughter-mother pictures of Susan (Bartlett) Sack and Harriet Bartlett. Susan, who was remembered as a skilled quill basket maker, was the wife of Henry Sack and mother of Michael Sack.

Harriet Bartlett
Millbrook, Nova Scotia, 1930

Johnson wrote that the women's clothing was of "considerable interest." He thought that the clothes were cut "nearly the same as that when only moose and caribou hides were available," and that the form, although not the style, were shared with other eastern Native groups.

Frederick Johnson's Work

Chris Morris with eels
Eskasoni, Nova Scotia, 1930

This image reflects older practices that are still part of Mi'kmaw communities. When Johnson designed the diorama of an Algonquian village eight years later at the Robert S. Peabody Museum, he modeled the eel rack, baskets and wigwam from those made by Chris and Mary Josephine Morris, shown here as well as in other images.

Mary Josephine (MacCleod) Morris
Eskasoni, Nova Scotia, 1930

The stories that Annie Claire Googoo says Johnson "just wanted to hear from the old people" were mostly about mystical aspects of Mi'kmaw life. They spoke about people's power regarding hunting, curing sickness, and determining everyday events like selling baskets and traveling from place to place. Other stories told of the formation of the world and of major geological events like earthquakes.

Frederick Johnson's Work

Chris and Mary Josephine Morris making a wigwam (pages 104 and 105) and wigwam interior (above) Eskasoni, Nova Scotia, 1930

Johnson photographed step-by-step as Chris and Mary Josephine made a wigwam, shown on pages 104 and 105. Wigwams were warm, dry and smoke free. Portable and water resistant, birch bark was a favorite choice not only for wigwams, but for other products as well. With both deerskin and a braided rug on the ground, the interior shown above reflects both age-old practices and newer ones. Tree branches mark the boundary of the hearth.

Mali A'n Morris and Peter Paul playing waltes
Eskasoni, Nova Scotia, 1930

In the inventory of the collection he made during his visits, Johnson wrote about waltes that it was "the most common game among the Micmac." Wapnaqnk, another dice game, he said was "exceedingly rare." His inventory summarizes the directions for how to play both waltes and wapnaqnk.

**Frederick Johnson
Lake Barriene, Quebec, 1929
Photographer unknown**

Fred Johnson was born in Everett, Massachusetts, in 1904 and died in Lowell, Massachusetts in 1994. Although less well known than many of his contemporaries, Fred's pioneering work remains a milestone in 20th century anthropology. This picture is one of many of him traveling to Native communities throughout northeastern North America.

As a boy Fred became acquainted with Frank G. Speck, an anthropologist and linguist from the University of Pennsylvania. With a strong interest in indigenous cultures and an aptitude for languages, Fred soon accompanied Speck on trips to Old Town, Maine, and then to other northeastern communities. Over a fifteen year period, Fred alternated schooling at Tufts University in Massachusetts and the University of Pennsylvania.

**Frederick Johnson
Annisquam River,
 Massachusetts, 1930
Photographer unknown**

Fred Johnson and Frank Speck
spent time during the
summer on the Annisquam River
in Massachusetts.

In 1936 Fred became the curator
at the Robert S. Peabody
Museum. He is remembered
particularly for his
interdisciplinary approaches to
archaeology. Among other work
throughout the Northeast, he
investigated a fish weir in
what is today the heart of
downtown Boston, bringing
new understanding to this 4,000
year old site.

Fred's energy and interests took
him in many other directions. In
addition to northeastern North
America, he did important field
work in the Yukon and Mexico.
His work with physicist Willard
Libby led to the development of
Carbon 14 dating, as a useful tool
for understanding the age of
ancient sites. He was a strong
believer in education and
helped to establish the Native
American Program at the Boston
Children's Museum.

Frederick Johnson's Work

**Archaeological Site
Merigomish, Nova Scotia, 1930**

People in this photograph probably are picking sweet hay, or sweet grass, which is known to grow in abundance in this spot.

Johnson's image label notes it as an archaeological site. There were no excavations during his visit, although the label and photograph suggest that he knew there were sites in the area. The artifact inventory from his visits include several stone tools from Merigomish that may have been collected from the surface of this site.

**Wide splint basket
Eskasoni, Nova Scotia, 1930**

The collection Johnson bought during his visits included clothing, baskets, boxes, hide scrapers, cradle boards, arrows, bows, pack straps, moccasins, brooches, beads, kettles, ladles, birch bark containers, snowshoes, netting needles, eel and seal spears, waltes and wapnaqnk games, and medicines. This collection is now curated at the National Museum of the American Indian, Smithsonian Institution, Washington, D.C.

Bridget (Prosper) Dennis and Mary Josephine Morris
Eskasoni, Nova Scotia, 1930

Bridget (Prosper) Dennis was married to Joe Dennis and was the sister of Peter, Mali and Jean Prosper. She was Wilfred Prosper's aunt, and has many grandchildren in Eskasoni today.

Mrs. J. Mitchell
Eskasoni, Nova Scotia, 1930

Mrs. J. Mitchell was not remembered during the community meeting at Eskasoni. She may have been visiting from Prince Edward Island, however, as Pictou Landing Saqamaw Albert Denny remembers Mitchells from Prince Edward Island at annual mawiomi and as classmates at Shubenacadie.

Frederick Johnson's Work

Salmon fishing with Joe "Amité" Jeddore
Miawpukek (Conne River), Newfoundland, 1931

In the past fish were a constant and dependable food source and they remain important today both economically and culturally. This sequence shows Joe catching salmon, an anadromous fish that runs in the spring and the fall. It is often called the premier fish in Atlantic Canada. Joes builds a rack, and smokes the fish in this sequence. Over millennia,

Mi'kmaq have used weirs, nets, spears, and hooks for catching fish. Besides salmon, eels were mentioned frequently during the community consultation in Miawpukek. John Nick Jeddore is known for his beautifully made eel spears, which are still used for night-fishing at the shoreline in Miawpukek.

Frederick Johnson's Work

Joe "Amité" Jeddore packing up camp Miawpukek (Conne River), Newfoundland, 1931

Joe Jeddore must have told Johnson quite a few stories while he was teaching him how to smoke fish and pack camp. Along with camping supplies, people carried whatever animals they had hunted or foods they had gathered in bundles like this, the canvas of which was also used as a tent. The "bundle" was made with a strap that measured from the elbow across the chest to the thumb. The head strap was measured from the elbow to the thumb. A mixture of rendered bear fat and berries is remembered as an important staple. In 1970 Lillian Marshall interviewed Michael Martin, who lived in Miawpukek until he was 13. He tells this story from his childhood about being out in the woods in Newfoundland:

We were about 100 miles out in the woods. We had a tent set up by the side of a lake. I didn't know how far out the other trappers were from us, but on Christmas afternoon, they came to visit us. There were many of us and my father built a great big fire and we had a lot of beavers. They set up two big round sticks alongside the fire and then the meat was strung up between the two poles. Then the people said prayers and sang hymns. Every once in a while, someone turned the meat over. When this meat was cooked, it was laid out on a big sheet of birchbark just like what we use for pizza today....We enjoyed this so much...

Frederick Johnson's Work

(pages 116 and 117)

Joe "Amité" Jeddore smoking
Miawpukek (Conne River),
  Newfoundland, 1931

Frederick Johnson with tripod
Pointe Bleu, Quebec, 1930

Thinking About the Seventh Generation

"If one of these people in these pictures came to the door, I wouldn't be surprised–I don't know why...to me they are real....these people are here."
Ben Martin

As the introduction of this book explains, between 1997 and 1999 the authors met with more than 40 Mi'kmaw Elders to talk about the people and places in these images. In this chapter Catherine Martin shares her experience of this process, and Johnson's photographs are intermingled with pictures from the communities today. Her words follow in italics throughout the chapter.

Creating an exhibition of Frederick Johnson's photographs was initially our objective and goal. However, the process of collecting information on these photographs, showing them to our Elders and listening to their stories, was the most significant to me. I was honored to be part of this journey of remembering and bringing these images back home to where they belong.

One of the most important messages that came from this experience was that our oral traditions are alive and well in the memories, the hearts and souls of our Elders. I have often spoken in the past about our living memories and how these living memories are a collective of our ancestors memories. I witnessed the sharing of living memories that were vivid and uncannily detailed. Those moments were sacred and unforgettable.

Wilfred Prosper and Caroline Marshall
Eskasoni, Nova Scotia, 1998
Photograph by Catherine Martin

Wilfred and Caroline examine the photographs during a community consultation at Eskasoni. Wilfred moved to Eskasoni from Chapel Island in 1947 during Centralization. He has been a prayer leader for 40 years, the Saqamaw at Eskasoni from 1956 to 1960, and a champion fiddler. Encouraged by his good friend Matthew Morris, son of Chris and Mary Josephine Morris, Wilfred put musical notation to ancient Mi'kmaw songs. Caroline Marshall was the wife of the late Donald Marshall Sr., who was Kji-Saqamaw. She has led an active life supporting and working with him.

I often thought how fortunate we were that so many of our Elders, our community experts, agreed to help out. They were our teachers, our mentors, and amazed us whenever we asked for their direction, advice and memories. Wherever we went we were welcomed. People heard about these photos and welcomed them in the same way as if they were welcoming long-lost relatives into their homes. It was a teaching for me, one that is embedded in me. Without them, there would be nothing to work with, nothing to bring these photos to life.

Levi Stride (left) and Aloysius Benoit Miawpukek (Conne River), Newfoundland, 1999 Photograph by Catherine Martin

Although Elder Levi Stride spent a good deal of his life in Glenwood, Newfoundland, the Stride family has been a part of the Miawpukek community for a long time. Levi works to increase the salmon population by enhancing the river system in Miawpukek. Aloysius Benoit is a great storyteller who has travelled to many places. Among other adventures, he survived two shipwrecks. He, like most people from Miawpukek, lives close to the land and has hunted and trapped all of his life.

Thinking About the Seventh Generation

Miawpukek (Conne River), Newfoundland, 1931 and 1999
Photographs by Frederick Johnson (above) and Leah Rosenmeier (right)

The current Saqamaw, Mi'sel Joe, explains that "it is different now than it used to be because we have to work harder to maintain our culture and traditional ways; things are too easy now, not like in the past. We have come from being very rich in our traditional ways to being very poor. We were rich in terms of living off the land, sharing, and we took care of each other even though we didn't have much money. Today, due to the land claim settlements and successful

economic initiatives in our community we have greater economic resources, but things have changed. Our community has prospered, grown, developed and the landscape has changed quite a bit. We have roads now and access to the outside world. We need to work towards greater balance in our lives and to keep our traditional values alive for the future."

Thinking About the Seventh Generation

**Madeline (Julien) Martin and Frank Julien
Millbrook, Nova Scotia, 1998
Photograph by Catherine Martin**

Madeline and Frank look at photographs during the community consultation at Millbrook. Madeline and Frank are brother and sister, children of Joe and Louise Julien. Joe Julien served as Saqamaw at Millbrook from 1916 to 1957. Madeline told us many stories about Charlie and Charlotte Wilmot, whose quilt she still has.

This affirmation of our living memories being so alive and well and intact gave me a sense of security. It made me want to show these photographs, with the tapes of the Elders laughing and remembering, to the world. I wanted to send this out to every skeptic, every academic, every high court judge and teacher, and show them that our living memory is valid. I am convinced that our oral histories remain intact, not in all of us, but in those who have been charged with this responsibility, who have been given this gift to remember.

Sarah (Nicholas) Francis
Pictou Landing, Nova Scotia, 1998
Photograph by Catherine Martin

Sarah (Nicholas) Francis, a member of the Pictou Landing Mi'kmaw Community, initiated a lot of the discussion when the curators traveled to Pictou Landing. Her statement that "People are always saying that Native people survived–No, I don't buy that. Oh we did more than just survive, my dear child–we *lived*," was a highlight of the community consultations. This quote is proudly displayed, along with some of the photographs, in The Confederacy of Mainland Mi'kmaq boardroom.

Sarah was band councillor of the Pictou Landing Band from 1969 to 1975.

Thinking About the Seventh Generation

Eskasoni, Nova Scotia, 1930 and 1999
Photographs by Frederick Johnson (above) and Leah Rosenmeier (right)

Established in 1832, Eskasoni has been occupied longer than any other contemporary Mi'kmaw community in Nova Scotia. With 3,250 band members, it has the largest population, and the greatest number of Mi'kmaq speakers.

Although some people returned to their own communities after the policy of Centralization was curtailed, many of the people who had moved to Eskasoni remained there.

Thinking About the Seventh Generation

Fred Sapier, Catherine Thomas, Martha and Frank Denny discuss photographs at the community meeting Pictou Landing, Nova Scotia, 1998
Photograph by Catherine Martin

Established in 1866, Pictou Landing is average size, with just under 500 people. Located on the coast, Pictou is tied closely to Merigomish Island, where Fred Sapier lives and where St. Anne's Day is celebrated. Marine resources have long been important to the community. After a sewage treatment plant polluted Boat Harbor in the 1960s, the community successfully sued the government for compensation and clean-up.

This memory is important to us today and in the future. It means we have what we need to reaffirm—to reclaim our land, our treaties, our language, our way of life. We have it and it needs to be shared, recorded and acknowledged. It is what our ancestors gave us to ensure that we had information for the future, for our children and generations to come. It is what our ancestors sent into the future for us to use today to reconnect our traditions, our ways, and to move into the new millennium.

Waycobah (Whycocomagh), Nova Scotia, 1930

The current Kji-Saqamaw, Ben Sylliboy, resides at the Waycobah First Nation, established in 1833. Centralization significantly impacted Waycobah, which by the late 1940s had nearly disappeared. Families moved back when Centralization was curtailed, however, and today it is one of the fastest growing communities in Nova Scotia.

Miawpukek (Conne River), Newfoundland, 1931 and 1999
Photographs by Frederick Johnson (above) and Leah Rosenmeier (right)

The building in the center foreground with the white roof was Nicholas Jeddore's cooper shop, where various wood products were made. Small green birch saplings were used to make barrels and also rings that attached sails to masts on schooners. Rinds from fir trees were gathered to line the hold in the schooners used to store fish. Saqamaw

Mi'sel Joe reports that in 1931 the Lake family moved into the village and built a sawmill with permission from the government but not the community. The sawmill operated alongside shops like the one operated by his great-grandfather Nicholas Jeddore, employing only a few people and using up locally available wood.

Most Mi'kmaw people do not use the past tense when they talk about people who have died, and when people think about the future, they focus on the seventh generation from the present. Knowledge about the past defines communities, and gives people strength and insight as new generations go about the work of building their futures. For many Mi'kmaq, museum objects and photographs such as these are not just "things" resting in cases and hanging on walls–in the contexts of living memory and human experience, they are meaningful and relevant aspects of present-day life.

Wula wi'Katikn ajipjutmek nutqo'ltijik wji kina'masultinew aqq wji nu'kwalsultinew apaja'tunew ta'n teli kina'muksi'kzpni'k Kniskamijinaqi'k. Nutqo'ltijik wpitnuaq etek elmi'knik ta'n teli Mi'knawimk.

**Jimmy Hennessey and Kevin Prosper
Pictou Landing, Nova Scotia, 1994
Photographer unknown**

On September 17, 1999 the Supreme Court of Canada found that the treaties of 1760-61 remained valid, and thereby reaffirmed the Mi'kmaq right to fish commercially. In the case, Regina v. Marshall, Canada's highest court found that Donald Marshall Jr. had a treaty right to fish for sustenance and earn a moderate livelihood from the commercial food fishery. On November 17th, 1999, in denying a motion for a stay, the Supreme Court issued a more detailed analysis of the commercial aspect of Regina v. Marshall.

Marissa Bernard, Emily Phillips, Mary Ann Martin, Autumn Cope, and Tiffany Kennedy at Millbrook's pow-wow
Millbrook, Nova Scotia, 2000
Photograph by T.J. Martin

The Mi'kmaq, like most other Native groups in eastern North America, have had European influences on their everyday lives for centuries. The last decade has been an important period of cultural renewal. Powwows are a time to celebrate through dance and feasting, and to teach children who they are and how their people have survived as a Nation. These young ladies from the Millbrook Mi'kmaw community take time out from the Millbrook powwow.

Thinking About the Seventh Generation

Virginia Knockwood, Patty Prosper and Jade Robinson Indian Brook, Nova Scotia, 1999
Photograph by Clayton Paul

A mother and grandmother to many, Geno Knockwood plays an important role in teaching young people. Her two young friends here are Patty Prosper of Waycobah and Jade Robinson of Indian Brook.

Geno was only 8 years old, a bit older than Jade Robinson in this photograph, when her family moved from Millbrook to Shubenacadie during Centralization. She remembers when she had to say goodbye to her best friend, Jean (Johnson) Martin. As they were packing up to get on the truck to go, Jean gave Geno a cat named Pepsi Cola in a brown bag to take with her, a promise that they would "stay best friends forever." Pepsi Cola, however, got away after they arrived at Shubenacadie and Geno remembers worrying that if Jean found out, their friendship would be ruined.

**Students visit the Nova Scotia Museum
Halifax, Nova Scotia, 1999
Photograph by Colin Bernard**

Student visitors to the exhibition *Mikwite'lmanej Mikmaqi'k: Let us Remember the Old Mi'kmaq*, which opened at the Nova Scotia Museum on September 30th, 1999. Many of these students are Mi'kmaq from the Millbrook Mi'kmaw Community and were excited to learn about their culture and heritage. As one of the Millbrook students put it, "This display is so true. It shows how life was for our people–I liked it."

Priorities for Mi'kmaw people in the 21st century center on securing recognition of aboriginal land title, revitalizing the Mi'kmaw language, strengthening cultural understanding and ceremonial practice, and increasing the capacity for self-determination. Sustaining economic development is integral to these goals. Mi'kmaw people of Nova Scotia continue to advance Mi'kmaw aboriginal and treaty rights in an effort to improve the economic status of the Mi'kmaw Nation. Major emphasis goes into revitalizing the language, one of the most important cultural aspects of the identity of any people.

The Federal and Provincial governments have been forced to recognize that historic treaties are still valid and are beginning to work with the Mi'kmaq on a nation-to-nation basis. With increased access to natural resources, the Mi'kmaq may once again enjoy economic sustainability.

Thinking About the Seventh Generation

Resources

Arneil, W.S.
1941
Memorandum summarizing results of investigation of the Indian reserves and administration to the premier of Nova Scotia. On file, The Confederacy of Mainland Mi'kmaq, Truro, N.S.

Camus, Tera
1999
"Mi'kmaq applaud apology," *The Halifax Herald Limited*, Halifax, N.S., March 22, 1999.

The Confederacy of Mainland Mi'kmaq, Native Council of Nova Scotia, and Union of of Nova Scotia Indians
2000
Mi'kmaw Resource Guide. Truro, N.S.: The Confederacy of Mainland Mi'kmaq.

Knockwood, Isabelle
1992
Out of the depths: the experiences of Mi'kmaw children at the Indian Residential School at Shubenacadie, Nova Scotia. Lockeport, N.S.: Roseway Publishing.

MacNeish, Richard S.
1996
"Frederick Johnson: 1904-1994," *American Antiquity* 61(2): 269-273.

Marshall, Murdena
1995
Mi'kmaq hieroglyphic prayers: readings in North America's first indigenous script. Halifax, N.S.: Nimbus Publishing.

Martin, Catherine
1991
Kwa'Nu'Te: Mi'kmaq and Maliseet Artists. Montreal: National Film Board of Canada.

1995
Mi'kmaq Family: Migmaoei Otjiosog. Montreal: National Film Board of Canada.

2000
Spirit Wind. Blind Bay, N.S.: Matues Productions.

Martin, Mike
n.d.
The hunter speaks and building a wigwam. Halifax, N.S.: Nova Scotia Department of Education and the Nova Scotia Museum.

Native Council of Nova Scotia
n.d.
Mi'kmaq language kits. Truro, N.S.: Native Council of Nova Scotia.

Nova Scotia Department of Education
n.d. *Mi'kmaq past and present: a resource guide.* Halifax, N.S.: Nova Scotia Department of Education.

Paul, Daniel
2000 *We were not the savages: a Mi'kmaq perspective of the collision between European and Native American Civilizations.* Halifax, N.S.: Fernwood Publishing.

Prins, Harald E. L.
1997 "'We fight with dignity': the Miawpukek Mi'kmaq quest for aboriginal rights in Newfoundland," *Papers of the Twenty-Eighth Algonquian Conference,* ed. David H. Pentland, Winnipeg: University of Manitoba, 283-305.

1996 *The Mi'kmaq: resistance, accommodation, and cultural survival.* Fort Worth, Tex.: Harcourt Brace College Publishers.

Wien, F. C.
1991 *Rebuilding the economic base of Indian communities: the Micmac in Nova Scotia.* Montreal, P.Q.: The Institute for Research on Public Policy/L'Institut de recherches politiques.

1983 *Socioeconomic characteristics of the Micmac in Nova Scotia.* Halifax, N.S.: Institute of Public Affairs, Dalhousie University.

Union of Nova Scotia Indians
1970-1971 *Research interviews with Elders.* On file at The Confederacy of Mainland Mi'kmaq, Truro, N.S.

Endnote
1. Ruth Holmes Whitehead, "A Brief Glimpse of Micmac Life: Objects from the McCord Collection," in *Wrapped in the Colours of the Earth: Cultural Heritage of the First Nations,* (Montreal: McCord Museum of Canadian History, 1992):77-83.

General Index

The Confederacy of Mainland Mi'kmaq in Truro, Nova Scotia, is a tribal council organization that provides advisory services to its six member Mi'kmaw bands. **Don Julien**, project advisor, is the Executive Director of The Confederacy of Mainland Mi'kmaq. **Tim Bernard** is the Manager of Eastern Woodland Publishing, a subsidiary of The Confederacy of Mainland Mi'kmaq. He served as project director, overseeing all aspects of the design and production of the book. **Art Stevens**, Graphic Designer at Eastern Woodland Publishing, designed the cover of the book and other graphic elements throughout the text as well as processing all photographic images. **Judy Works**, Prepress Designer at Eastern Woodland Publishing, set the type and was patient through many drafts. **Mary Sylliboy** assisted during the community visitations with our Elders, translating and photographing.

The **Robert S. Peabody Museum of Archaeology** is located at Phillips Academy in Andover, Massachusetts. **James W. Bradley** has been the director since 1990. The museum is dedicated to teaching the science of archaeology and to understanding and preserving the cultures of Native American people. **Leah Rosenmeier** is the Outreach and Repatriation Coordinator at the Museum and served as project coordinator for the book. She worked with Tim Bernard and Catherine Martin to write and design the book.

Catherine Martin, an independent filmmaker and researcher, now works at the Native Counseling Unit at Dalhousie University, Halifax, Nova Scotia. She worked closely with members of the project team, writing stories and keeping Miawpukek (Conne River) and Pictou Landing connected to the project.

Murdena Marshall is an Elder, historian and linguist, who served as a project advisor. Among much else, she was the primary liaison with Eskasoni and worked closely with Patsy Paul Martin on the Mi'kmaw translations.